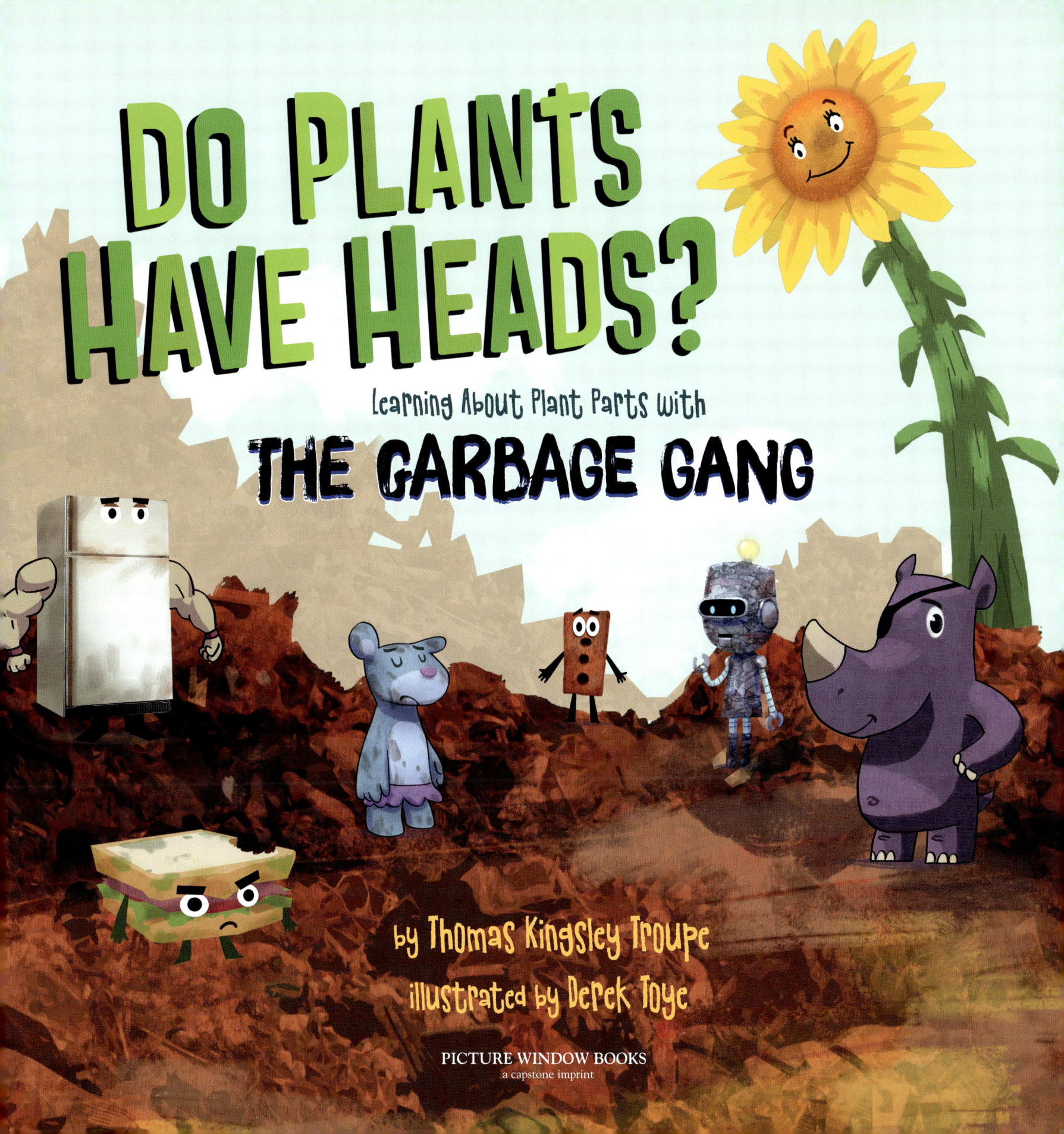

MEET THE GARBAGE GANG:

SAM HAMMWICH
Sam is a once-delicious sandwich that has a bit of lettuce and tomato. He is usually crabby and a bit of a loudmouth.

GORDY
Gordy is a small rhino who wears an eyepatch even though he doesn't need one. He lives in the city dump. His friends don't visit him in the smelly dump, so Gordy created his own friends—the Garbage Gang!

SOGGY
Soggy is a stuffed bear from a carnival game. She fell into a puddle of dumpster juice and has never been the same.

RICK
Rick is a brick. He is terrified of bugs, especially bees, which is odd … since he's a brick.

CANN-DEE
Cann-Dee is a robot made of aluminum cans. She can pull random facts out of thin air.

MR. FRIGID
Mr. Frigid is a huge refrigerator that sprouted arms and legs. He doesn't say much, but he's super strong.

CLUNK!

"Whoa! What was that?"

"Sorry about that. I lost one of my seeds!"

"What's the seed for? Do you need it back?"

"Oh, no! Seeds are how sunflowers and other plants are created."

"Are you trying to tell me there's a big ol' flower like you stuffed in there? What a load of dill!"

"Remember how I was telling you that I create food for myself through photosynthesis?"

"Sure, we remember."

"Well, water comes up through my stem, moves into the leaves, and spreads out."

"Sunlight plus water in your leaves equals food?"

"Almost. My leaves also absorb carbon dioxide."

"Yes, there was a little plant in there."

"That's right. My flower, or head, is where that seed was made."

"Guys! Look at all of the sunflower seeds in Raye's face! They're everywhere."

"Random fact nugget loaded: A sunflower has between 800 and 2,000 seeds in its flower."

Did you ever wonder why flowers are so pretty and colorful?

"Not really."

"Ignore him, Raye, I've always wondered!"

"Are flowers colorful to make the other plants feel bad?"

"Maybe a rainbow smashed into them or something."

"Colors ... nice."

"All great guesses, guys, but none of them are correct. Bright colors bring out our busiest and buzziest helpers."

"Oh, no. Don't even tell me!"

"Bees!"

"This isn't good!"

"Bees love the bright colors on our petals. The fragrance in flowers helps attract bees to us."

"Any fragrance is better than the smell of garbage!"

"Mr. Frigid? Where are you? Please hide me!"

"So, why would you want bees to stop by? Aren't they busy making honey?"

"Yeah, why? Tell them to get outta here!"

19

Glossary

carbon dioxide—a colorless, odorless gas that people and animals breathe out; plants take in carbon dioxide because they need it to survive

flower—the colorful part of a plant that makes seeds and fruit

nectar—a sweet liquid found in many flowers

nutrients—parts of food, like vitamins, that are needed for growth

oxygen—a colorless gas in the air that people breathe; humans and animals need oxygen to live

petal—one of the colored outer parts of a flower

photosynthesis—a process plants use to make food and oxygen

pistil—female reproductive part in a flower

pollen—a powder made by flowers to help them create new seeds

pollination—the process of carrying pollen from the stamen to the pistil

soil—another word for dirt

stamen—the male part of a flower that makes pollen

stem—the part of the plant that connects the roots to the leaves

You're looking up words? That's one smart move, kid!

Read More

Lynette, Rachel. *Plants*. The Science Behind. Chicago: Raintree, 2012.

Sterling, Kristin. *Exploring Flowers*. Let's Look at Plants. Minneapolis: Lerner Publications, 2012.

Waldron, Melanie. *Seeds and Fruits*. Plant Parts. Chicago: Heinemann Library, 2014.

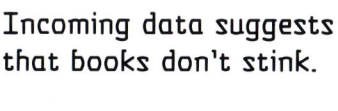

Incoming data suggests that books don't stink.

Critical Thinking Using the Common Core

1. Name three plant parts and list their functions. Are human body parts similar or different? (Integration of Knowledge and Ideas)

2. What important role do bees and other insects play in pollination? (Key Ideas and Details)

Index

bees, 18, 19, 20, 21, 22
carbon dioxide, 12, 13
flowers, 15, 16, 17, 18, 20, 21
fruits, 16, 17, 20
heads, 6, 14, 15, 22
leaves, 10, 11, 12, 20
nectar, 20, 21
oxygen, 13, 20
petals, 19, 20
photosynthesis, 11–13
pistils, 20
pollen, 20, 21
pollination, 20, 21
roots, 8, 9, 10
seeds, 7, 8, 15, 16, 17, 20
soil, 8, 9, 13
stamens, 20
stems, 10, 12
sunlight, 11, 13
water, 9, 12, 13

Internet Sites

FactHound offers a safe, fun way to find Internet sites related to this book. All of the sites on FactHound have been researched by our staff.

Here's all you do:

Visit www.facthound.com

Type in this code: 9781479570591

Super-cool stuff! Check out projects, games and lots more at www.capstonekids.com

Thanks to our advisers for their expertise, research, and advice:
Christopher T. Ruhland, PhD
Professor of Biological Sciences
Department of Biology
Minnesota State University, Mankato

Editor: Shelly Lyons
Designer: Aruna Rangarajan
Creative Director: Nathan Gassman
Production Specialist: Lori Barbeau
The illustrations in this book were created digitally.

Picture Window Books are published by Capstone,
1710 Roe Crest Drive, North Mankato, Minnesota 56003
www.capstonepub.com

Copyright © 2016 by Picture Window Books, a Capstone imprint. All rights reserved. No part of this publication may be reproduced in whole or in part, or stored in a retrieval system, or transmitted in any form or by any means, electronic, mechanical, photocopying, recording, or otherwise, without written permission of the publisher.

Library of Congress Cataloging-in-Publication Data
Troupe, Thomas Kingsley, author.
Do plants have heads? : learning about plant parts with the Garbage Gang / by Thomas Kingsley Troupe.
pages cm. — (Picture Window books. The Garbage Gang's super science questions)
Summary: "Humorous text and characters teach kids about plant parts"— Provided by publisher.
Audience: Ages 5-7
Audience: K to grade 3
Includes bibliographical references and index.
ISBN 978-1-4795-7059-1 (library binding)
ISBN 978-1-4795-7069-0 (eBook pdf)
1. Plant physiology—Juvenile literature. 2. Plants—Juvenile literature. 3. Plants—Development—Juvenile literature. 4. Botany—Juvenile literature. I. Title.
QK711.5.T76 2016
580—dc23   2014049607
        Printed in the United States of America in
        North Mankato, Minnesota.
        102015   009295R

Look for all the books in the series:

Are Bowling Balls Bullies? Learning About Forces and Motion with **THE GARBAGE GANG**

Do Ants Get Lost? Learning About Animal Communication with **THE GARBAGE GANG**

Do Bees Poop? Learning About Living and Nonliving Things with **THE GARBAGE GANG**

Do Plants Have Heads? Learning About Plant Parts with **THE GARBAGE GANG**

What's With the Long Naps, Bears? Learning About Hibernation with **THE GARBAGE GANG**

Why Do Dead Fish Float? Learning About Matter with **THE GARBAGE GANG**

Why Does My Body Make Bubbles? Learning About the Digestive System with **THE GARBAGE GANG**

You Call That A Nose? Learning About Human Senses with **THE GARBAGE GANG**

More books! Are you kidding me? This is the best news since sliced bread!

Seriously?